GIFTED
&
TALENTED®

*To develop
your child's gifts
and talents*

STORY STARTERS

Stories About Me

By Diane Cuneo

Illustrated by Kerry Manwaring

Lowell 🏠 House
Juvenile
Los Angeles

CONTEMPORARY BOOKS
Chicago

Manufactured in the United States of America

ISBN: 1-56565-242-8

10 9 8 7 6 5

GIFTED AND TALENTED® STORY STARTERS: Stories About Me will help develop your child's natural talents and gifts by providing story-telling and writing activities to enhance critical and creative thinking skills. These skills of logic and reasoning teach children **how to think**. They are precisely the skills emphasized by teachers of gifted and talented children. Here are some of the skills you will find:

- Deduction — the ability to reach a logical conclusion by interpreting clues

- Understanding Relationships — the ability to recognize how objects, shapes, and words are similar or dissimilar; to classify or categorize

- Sequencing — the ability to organize events, numbers; to recognize patterns

- Inference — the ability to reach logical conclusions from given or assumed evidence

- Creative Thinking —the ability to generate unique ideas; to compare and contrast the same elements in different situations; to present imaginative, numerous solutions to problems; to develop or expand on ideas, stories, or illustrations

Stories About Me is a unique, customized writing exercise book that is as much about self-discovery as it is about creativity. The less you try to shape the outcome of these exercises, the more this book will truly be "about" your child. Remember that there is no "right" way to perform any of the activities in this book. If your child needs help understanding an exercise, try to give the child options rather than answers. For example, in one of the Beginning Exercises, the child is asked to compare the color of his or her eyes to something else in a simile sentence: "My eyes are as _____ as a _____ ." You can help your child by listing various items you can think of that match, such as "brown as a walnut, a piece of toast, or a tree trunk." Ask the child to add to your examples, then choose one he or she likes. It is important not to be judgmental about your child's choices, as he or she should not form too narrow or too rigid a concept of "proper" descriptions.

In the Beginning Exercises, the child can record facts about his or her life by choosing answers from provided lists, or by filling in the blanks with his or her own answers. The early exercises will help prepare your child for Eye-Opening Descriptive Exercises, which will encourage your child to take notes and to pay more attention to his or her environment. These exercises will also stimulate your child's imagination. By following the examples provided, the child will learn how to mine personal feelings, experiences, and observations to create unique, one-of-a-kind stories. Work with your child and use questions to guide your child to find his or her own answers. Going over all the exercises with your child will reinforce not only the function of language but its richness as well.

Many of the Eye-Opening Descriptive Exercises take what is familiar and ask unusual questions, which lead the child to delve deeper into the essence of his or her favorite things, such as games, foods, movies, or books. Perspective is also explored in this section, as the child is asked to discuss familiar places, then look at them again from a view other than his or her own; for example, as a bug, a vacuum cleaner, or a ketchup bottle! The child must pretend to be that object, and physically acting out that role will help your child try to understand and write about the object's point of view.

Once the child has recorded story ideas in the Eye-Opening Descriptive Exercises, he or she can move on to What If . . . ? and Imagine Exercises, in which the child is prompted to complete creative writing activities and draw accompanying pictures in which the child is the star. Here, children can imagine themselves as a chef, a superhero, or even the president!

These creative exercises will enable children to begin more complex story-telling in Write the Middle and Write the Ending Exercises. Here, stories are started for the child, and the child then has to provide either the middle or the end. In many cases, the beginnings are peppered with blank spaces, allowing the child to fill in personal facts to make the stories truly "about" him or her. Show your child how the information recorded in the earlier exercises can be used to fill in the story lines of these later stories.

To help your child through the middle exercises, remember that the middle of a story is a link that provides a logical chain of events from the beginning (provided) to the end (provided). Ask the child to read the ending out loud and imagine what could have happened to lead to such an end. To help your child through the ending exercises, ask him or her to imagine more than one way the story can conclude. The more children use their imaginations, the more they will move away from clichéd endings and into creative endings.

The final section contains Advanced Exercises. These provide little help in the creation and writing of each story. The child is given scenarios for stories, but unlike the other exercises, no portion of a story is provided. Some pages are even left blank for the child to create truly original stories. Please encourage your child to consider his or her initial effort as a first draft. Once some time has passed, ask the child to expand on the first attempt on another piece of paper. You will both be surprised at how effortlessly the second (and third) drafts become more complete, and even more interesting, stories.

Participate with and read to your child. Help him or her with harder words. A child's imagination should not be limited only to those words he or she can read, since children understand the meaning of words even if they cannot read them. The same is true for those words they cannot write. If necessary, record your child's stories for him or her. Regardless of whether your child can write full, complete sentences, your child will gain much from this book. Exercising the imagination is what **GIFTED & TALENTED® STORY STARTERS** is all about.

Good luck, have fun, and remember: good writers read, so go to the library often with your child.

The following exercises will help you write stories about yourself. Fill in the blanks, circle the answers, or check the boxes to complete each one.

My name is _____. I am _____ years old! On my next birthday, I will have this many candles on my cake:

drawn by _____

Circle one word for each answer below.

I am **older** **younger** than the ancient pyramids in Egypt.
I am **older** **younger** than a baby.
I am **older** **younger** than the leftovers in our refrigerator!

I am _____ feet and _____ inches tall.

Draw a check mark in the box next to one answer, or make up an answer of your own!

I am as tall as

❑ a skyscraper
☑ a tree
❑ a parking meter
❑ a fire hydrant
❑ a dandelion
❑ _____

I weigh _____ pounds.

If you want to know how heavy that is, just lift

❑ a balloon
❑ an elephant
☑ a bucket of water
❑ a house
❑ a butterfly
❑ _____

My eyes are the color ___*is*___. Here is a picture of them.

drawn by ✏ _____

Here is a list of things that are the same color as my eyes.

my eyes are circle
a baset ball
is circle

Try to write a creative sentence by following the example below.

Example: My eyes are as **yellow** as a **banana**.

My eyes are as ___*white*___ as a ___*Walls*___.

My hair is ___*black*___.

Here is a list of things I can think of that are the same color as my hair.

Pant are Black
Bag are Black
eye Brow

My hair is the color of ___*Black*___.

My hair is as ___*Black*___ as a ___*Black Bag*___.

I go to _____ God's kid's Academy _____ School.
Here is a picture of it.

draw by _____

My teacher's name is _____ Ms Rhone _____.

My best friend at school's name is _ Solomon _____.

At school, I like to read

☑ **funny stories**   ☑ **scary stories**

☑ **sad stories**   ☐ **weird stories**

☐ **everything**   ☐ _____

I write about a lot of things at school. But this is a book about ME! Here is a picture of me at school.

draw by _____

The following exercises will help you write about your feelings.

When I am happy, I feel like

❑ **a bubble**

❑ **a circus**

❑ _____

☑ **a puppy**

☑ **a sunny day**

Here is a picture of me when I feel happy.

drawn by _____

Some things that make me feel happy are:

When my mothe Do not hit me, and Thow away my toys,

When I am silly, I feel like

☑ a clown

☐ a bouncing ball

☑ a wiggly worm

☐ a cartoon character

☐ _____

Here is a picture of me when I feel silly.

drawn by _____

Some things that make me feel silly are:

When I wiggly litk a worm.

When I am mad, I feel like

☑ **a lightning bolt**

☐ **a stick of dynamite**

☐ **a snorting bull**

☐ **a boiling pot**

☐ _____

Here is a picture of me when I feel mad.

I not leo

drawn by _____

Some things that make me feel mad are:

When mother hit me
and thow away my toys.

When I am sad, I feel like

❏ **a rainy day**

☑ **a sad song**

❏ **a flat balloon**

❏ **a dirty sock**

❏ _____

Here is a picture of me when I feel sad.

drawn by _____

Some things that make me feel sad are:

_____

_____

_____

_____

_____

Fill in the blanks on the next few pages. When you write, it is important to use your imagination! Here is an example.

My favorite toy is **my jump rope**.

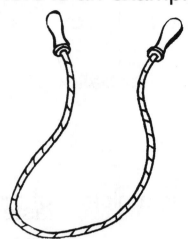

My favorite toy tastes like **lettuce**.
My favorite toy smells like **summer**.
My favorite toy looks like **a snake**.
My favorite toy feels like **a porcupine**.
My favorite toy sounds like **hiccups**.

My favorite sport is _____Base ball_____.

drawn by _____

My favorite sport tastes like ___Base ball___.
My favorite sport smells like ___is foot ball___.
My favorite sport looks like ___soccoer ball___.
My favorite sport feels like ___is volleyball___.
My favorite sport sounds like _____.

My favorite food is _____.

drawn by _____

My favorite food tastes like _____.
My favorite food smells like _____.
My favorite food looks like _____.
My favorite food feels like _____.
My favorite food sounds like _____.

My favorite color is _____.

drawn by _____

My favorite color tastes like _____.
My favorite color smells like _____.
My favorite color looks like _____.
My favorite color feels like _____.
My favorite color sounds like _____.

My favorite feeling is _____.

drawn by _____

My favorite feeling tastes like _____.
My favorite feeling smells like _____.
My favorite feeling looks like _____.
My favorite feeling feels like _____.
My favorite feeling sounds like _____.

My favorite day is _____.

drawn by _____

My favorite day tastes like _____.
My favorite day smells like _____.
My favorite day looks like _____.
My favorite day feels like _____.
My favorite day sounds like _____.

On pages 10 to 13 in this book, you wrote about what you feel like when you are happy, silly, mad, and sad. Now use what you wrote there to complete this story.

A FUNNY FEELING

By _____

   I was having a very good day. In the morning, I got to have my favorite breakfast, _____. I wasn't late for school, and I got to do my favorite thing, which is _____. My best friend, _____, said I could come over that afternoon and play. I felt so happy, I turned into a _____. That made me feel silly, and suddenly I turned into a _____! I was starting to get mad, and then I turned into a _____. It was becoming a bad day! That made me feel sad, and all of a sudden I turned into a _____!

   It was getting to be ridiculous! So I said some magic words that only I know. They went like this: _____, _____, _____!

And everything went back to normal, thank goodness!

The End

17

The name of my favorite fairy tale is _____

_____.

My favorite fairy tale is

❑ **funny**

❑ **scary**

❑ **weird**

❑ **sad**

❑ **silly**

❑ _____

If I were in my favorite fairy tale, I would be _____

_____.

I would look like this:

drawn by _____

If I were in my favorite fairy tale, it would end

❑ **the same way**   ❑ **a different way**

Here is the way it would end:

_____

_____

_____

_____

_____

The name of my favorite movie is _____

_____ .

My favorite movie is:

❏ **funny**   ❏ **sad**

❏ **scary**   ❏ **silly**

❏ **weird**   ❏ _____

If I were in my favorite movie, I would be _____

_____ .

If I were in my favorite movie, it would end

❏ **the same way**   ❏ **a different way**

Here is how it would end:

_____

_____

_____

_____

_____

_____

_____

For the following exercises, fill in the blanks. Look carefully around you before you write your answers.

My room at home is _____.

The best thing in my room is _____.

It has _____ window(s).

It has _____ door(s).

The walls are the color _____.

Here is a list of things in my room. Some of them are hanging on my walls.

_____   _____

_____   _____

_____   _____

_____   _____

_____   _____

_____   _____

Here is a picture of my room. I have drawn everything in it!

drawn by _____

If you were a bug in your room, things would look different to you! Things would sound and feel different, too! Your room might look like this to a bug:

drawn by _____

Pretend that you are a bug. Write all about
what your room would look like, sound
like, feel like, smell like, and taste
like to a bug.

This room is _____! It looks

_____.

I can hear _____ and _____

_____.

The carpet is so deep! It _____

_____.

I can smell _____. I can also smell_____

_____.

This _____ on the carpet tastes _____.

It is_____

_____

_____

_____

_____

_____

_____

_____

_____

_____

_____.

Make a list of the foods in your refrigerator. Add some pictures of them to the shelves.

Imagine what it would feel like to be a ketchup bottle in your refrigerator. The ketchup sure spends a lot of time there! How does the ketchup bottle feel about the other foods in the refrigerator? Write your story ideas on the lines below.

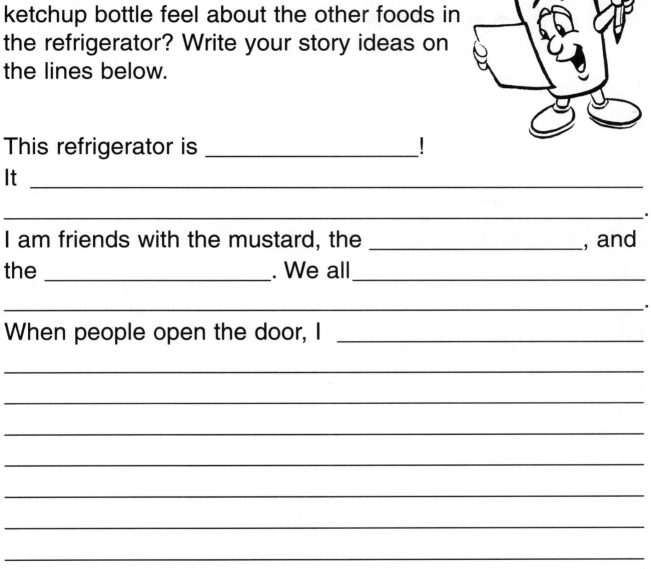

This refrigerator is _____!

It _____

_____.

I am friends with the mustard, the _____, and the _____. We all_____

_____.

When people open the door, I _____

_____

_____

_____

_____

_____

_____

_____

_____

_____

_____.

Think about your classroom at school. Write your answers on the lines below.

My classroom at school is _____. It has _____ windows. It has _____ cubbies for everyone's things. It has _____ desks. Hanging on the walls of my classroom are pictures of _____ and _____, and there is also a _____.

Here is a picture of my classroom. I tried to draw everything in it!

drawn by _____

My favorite part of the room is _____.
My favorite subject is _____. I enjoy learning all about _____.

Imagine if your classroom were on the moon! Things float on the moon, because there is less gravity to hold them down. How different would school be on the moon? Write all about it on the lines below.

On the moon, I can _____ during recess. There are a lot of big holes on the moon, so playing _____ with my classmates is a lot of fun! If I want the teacher to call on me, I don't just raise my hand, I _____! There is no air to breathe on the moon, so my classmates and I have to _____. If I get bored in school, sometimes I can look out the window and see the Earth. It looks like _____. Here are some more reasons why going to school on the moon is so different than going to school on Earth:

_____

_____

_____

_____

_____

_____

_____

On the following pages, use your imagination to fill in the blanks. It's fun to imagine yourself as different things.

If I were an animal, I would be a _____.

Why? Because I _____

_____

_____

_____

_____

_____

If I were a letter of the alphabet, I would be _____.

Why? Because I _____

_____

_____

_____

_____

_____

If I were a fruit, I would be a _____.

Why? Because I _____

_____

_____

_____

_____

_____

If I were a ball, I would be a _____.

Why? Because I _____

_____

_____

_____

_____

_____

If I were a grown-up, I would be a _____.

Why? Because I _____

_____

_____

_____

_____

_____

If I were a musical instrument, I would be a _____.

Why? Because I _____

_____

_____

_____

_____

_____

If I were a plant, I would be a _____.

Why? Because I _____

_____

_____

_____

_____

_____

If I were a food, I would be a _____.

Why? Because I _____

_____

_____

_____

_____

If I were a superhero, my name would be _____.

I would help to protect _____ and _____.

People would _____ as I _____ by.

I would have a cool superhero costume! I would wear _____ and _____. The colors in my costume would be _____ and _____.

As a superhero, I would have lots of special powers! Here is a list of what my special powers would be:

_____   _____

_____   _____

_____   _____

_____   _____

_____   _____

_____   _____

I would need special equipment to help me be a superhero. Here is a list of some of my things:

_____   _____

_____   _____

_____   _____

_____   _____

_____   _____

_____   _____

Here's a picture of me wearing my cool superhero costume.

drawn by ✏ _____

The picture on the opposite page is full of interesting things. Pick one part of that picture and write your own story about it below, with you as a superhero.

_____

_____

_____

_____

_____

_____

_____

_____

_____

_____

_____

_____

_____

_____

_____

_____

_____

_____

_____

_____

The picture on the opposite page is full of interesting things. Pick one part of that picture and write your own story about it below, with you as a superhero.

_____

_____

_____

_____

_____

_____

_____

_____

_____

_____

_____

_____

_____

_____

_____

_____

_____

_____

_____

Here, draw a comic-book story that stars you as a superhero!

drawn by

You may have read stories about people who can talk to animals. It is fun to imagine what an animal might say to you. But it is also fun to imagine what other things might say. On the next few pages, write your ideas on the lines.

If a vacuum cleaner could talk to me, here is what it might say:

"
_____
_____
_____
_____
                                                    "
_____

If a pickle could talk to me, here is what it might say:

"
_____
_____
_____
                                                    "
_____

If a baseball could talk to me, here is what it might say:
"

_____

_____

_____

_____
"
_____

If a crack in the sidewalk could talk to me, here is what it might say:
"

_____

_____

_____

_____
"
_____

If a bathtub could talk to me, here is what it might say:

"

_____

_____

_____

_____

"

_____

If a fly could talk to me, here is what it might say:

"

_____

_____

_____

"

_____

If my alarm clock could talk to me, here is what it might say:

"_____

_____

_____

_____
                                                 "
_____

If my lunch box could talk to me, here is what it might say:

"_____

_____

_____

_____
                                                 "
_____

Fill in the blanks of this story. On the next page, draw a picture to go with the story. Use your imagination!

THE BEST PLAYGROUND IN THE WORLD
By _____

One morning I was eating my favorite breakfast of _____ when I heard a knock _____. When my mom and I opened it, a man in a _____ and a _____ was standing there. He was holding a rolled-up _____ of _____.

"Are you _____?" he asked.

"Yes, _____," I said.

"I heard you have a good imagination," said _____. "So I would like you to help me build the perfect playground. You can draw the plans on _____."

"Can I do anything I want?" I asked, still chewing on my _____.

"_____," he said.

"Can I design a slide that makes you go _____ miles an hour, for _____ miles? Can I design a swing that _____? Or a place to play _____?"

"Sure!" he said. "And we'll give you a year's supply of your favorite snack food."

"I'll do it," I said. "I love _____!"

The End

Do a drawing of the plan you made for the playground. Also, make a list of the cool things you put in the playground.

drawn by _____

_____   _____

_____   _____

_____   _____

Imagine that you are the owner and head chef of a fancy restaurant. Complete the menu by making a list of the foods you will serve there. You are in charge! Write the name of your restaurant on the line below.

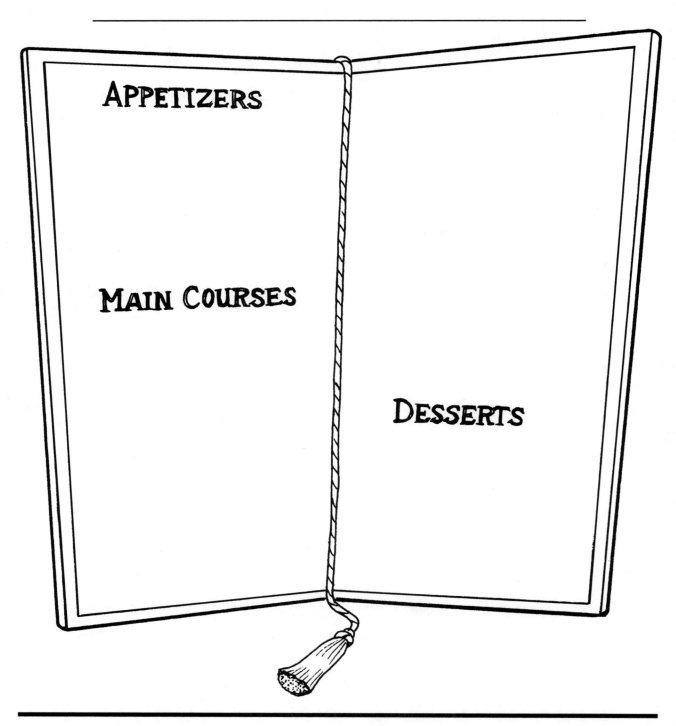

Imagine that you are elected President of the United States! Make a list of laws that you want people to follow. The first one has been started for you.

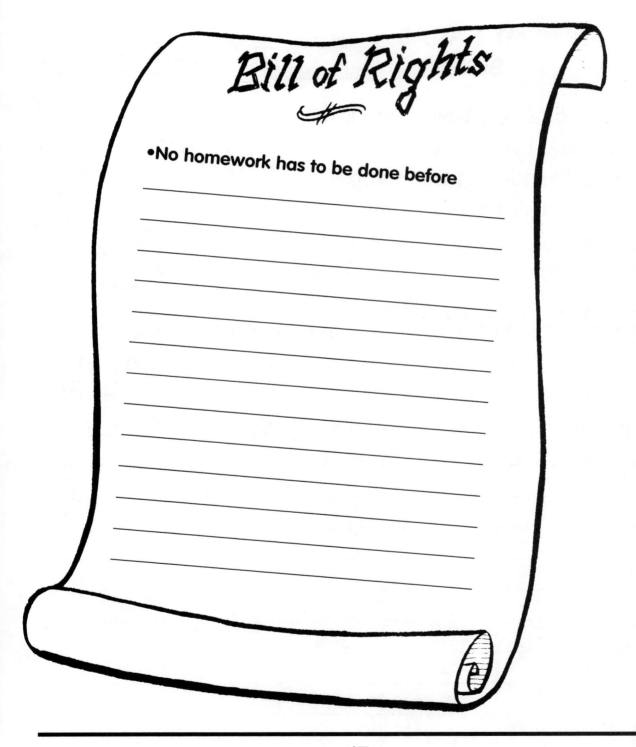

Bill of Rights

•No homework has to be done before

On page 29 of this book, you wrote about your favorite type of ball and why you would like to be that ball. Use what you wrote to complete this story. When you are finished, draw a picture of what you would look like as a ball.

MY DAY AS A _____
By _____

Have you ever woken up in the morning and not felt quite the same? One morning that happened to me. I felt like I was a funny shape, a _____ shape. I looked at my skin, and it was covered with _____ and the color of _____.
I tried to get out of bed. When I hit the floor, I made a _____ sound! I _____ to the mirror, and was I shocked! I was a ball! A _____, to be exact!

Here is what happened to me that day. First, I_____

_____

_____

_____

_____

_____

_____

_____

_____

_____

_____

_____

_____

_____

_____

_____

_____

_____

_____

_____

_____

The End

Here is a picture of me that day.

drawn by _____

On the following pages, you will find the beginnings of stories. Fill in the blanks and write the endings. Be sure to use facts about yourself to make the stories good.

TEACHER FOR A DAY

By _____

We were sitting in class one day, waiting for our teacher, _____. It was getting late. We waited and waited. Some kids were not behaving. They were _____. I wanted the teacher to get there soon because it was time for my favorite subject, _____. Suddenly, the principal came into the room.

"Your teacher is out sick today. One of you will have to teach the class," the principal said. And then, to my surprise, she picked ME!

I went up to the front of the class and sat at my teacher's desk. Then _____

_____

_____

_____

_____

_____

_____

_____

_____

_____

_____

_____

_____

_____

_____

_____

_____

_____

The End

Here is a picture of me as the teacher!

drawn by _____

A STRANGER IN THE MIRROR
By _____

I was walking to my friend's house one day. It was the kind of day I liked, because it was _____. I was humming my favorite song, _____, and thinking about what my best friend, _____, would want to do when I got there. On the way I passed a store window. I looked in it, and something seemed strange.

When I got to my friend's house, my friend screamed. I looked in the mirror. The person looking back wasn't me! I have _____ hair, and the person in the mirror had _____ hair. I have _____ eyes, and the person in the mirror had _____ eyes. And worst of all, I have only one nose, and the person in the mirror had _____ noses!

My friend said, "That's weird!" What was going on? I wondered. My friend and I _____

_____

_____

_____

_____

_____

_____

_____

The End

Here is a picture of the strange person I saw in the mirror!

drawn by ✐ _____

TIME FLIES BACKWARD

By _____

I always look at a clock at night, because my bedtime is _____ o'clock. At my house, we have _____ clocks. One night as I was going to bed, they all started running backward!

I was just about to go to sleep, when I felt my body getting out of bed! It felt like someone was picking me up! I took off my pajamas and put on a robe. Suddenly, my hair was wet, and I was walking backward into the bathroom! And as I stood by the tub, the water began to come up through the drain to fill the tub! And that was just the beginning!

Next _____

_____

_____

_____

_____

_____

_____

_____

_____

_____

_____

_____

_____

_____

_____

_____

The End

Here is a picture of what happened.

drawn by _____

On the following pages, the beginnings and endings of each story have been done for you. Use your imagination to write all the middle parts of the stories.

HEAD IN THE CLOUDS

By _____

On summer days, I like to be outside playing _____. Well, that is exactly what I was doing one day when a strange thing happened. I started to float! I weigh _____ pounds and am not used to floating. At first I was only one inch off the ground. Then I was hanging about three feet off the ground! My friends _____ and _____ were staring at me.

"What are you staring at?" I said.
"You're floating up to the sky!" they cried.
And so I was! I started to _____

_____

_____

_____

_____

_____

_____

_____

_____

_____

_____

_____

_____

_____

_____

_____

_____

_____

Before we knew it, my friends and I began moving slowly back down toward the ground. We had been gone for seven hours, and it was getting dark! I don't know how we flew that day, but I hope we do it again!

The End

Here is a picture of me with my head in the clouds.

drawn by _____

IF EVERY DAY WERE _____ DAY

By _____

There are seven days in a week: Monday, Tuesday, Wednesday, Thursday, Friday, Saturday, and Sunday. But my favorite day is _____. Why? Because _____

_____.

If I could be in charge of making every day of the week _____day, I would be very happy! Here's how my week would go. First, I'd wake up and remember that today is _____day. Then I would _____

_____

_____

_____

_____

_____

_____

_____

_____

_____

_____

_____

_____

_____

_____

_____

_____

_____

_____

_____

Some people might beg me to change the day to another day, but I don't think I would. Unless they said, "_____." Then maybe I would change it to my second favorite day, which is _____!

The End

Here is a picture of me on my favorite day of the week.

drawn by _____

THE DAY I SAVED LITTLE RED

By _____

One day I happened to be
strolling through the forest, and who
do you think I bumped into? Little
Red Riding Hood! She was carrying
a basket of food.

"Hello," she said.

"Hello," I said. "Don't you know you're not supposed to
talk to strangers?"

"Well, yes," she said. "But you seem so very nice."

"I am," I said. "But there's a big, bad wolf down the path
waiting for you, and he's not nice at all!"

"Oh!" she squealed. "What should I do?"

So I came up with a plan. First, _____

_____

_____

_____

_____

_____

_____

_____

_____

_____

_____

_____

_____

_____

_____

_____

_____

_____

_____

And, because of my plan, the wolf changed his ways and got a job as a lifeguard. Little Red Riding Hood got her hood back, and she still wears it every day. Granny used the green apples we rolled on the floor to make ten pies, and I ate seven of them!

The End

Here is a picture of me with Little Red.

drawn by _____

MY FAVORITE BOOK AND ME
By _____

My favorite book is _____.
I like it because _____.
I was reading this book one day when I
tripped and fell into it! One second I was
holding the book, and the next second I
was IN the book! I fell in at the part where
_____. Then I became
a part of the story!

Here is what happened: _____

_____

_____

_____

_____

_____

_____

_____

_____

_____

_____

_____

_____

_____

_____
_____
_____
_____
_____
_____
_____
_____

Then I heard someone calling my name from outside the book. It was my _____. And POOF! I was out of the story, and just in time, too!

The End

Here is a picture of me in my favorite book.

drawn by ✏ _____

THE TALKING BATHTUB

By _____

One day I was taking a bath, getting wrinkled as a
_____. I had my favorite toy in the tub with me,
my _____. I was having a good old time splashing
and playing when I heard a strange voice.

"MMMmfptttt!" it said.

"What?" I said.

"MMMmPFFphitthift!" it said.

The sound seemed to be
coming from the bathtub drain,
so I pulled out the plug.

"That's better," the voice said.
"It's hard to talk with a big plug in
your mouth."

"Yes, I'm sure it is," I said, trying to be polite. Then I ____

_____

_____

_____

_____

_____

_____

_____

_____

_____

_____

_____

_____

_____

_____

_____

_____

_____

"Where have you been?" Mom said crossly.

"In the tub," I said.

"You weren't there when I looked before!" she said. She was mad!

I did not think Mom would like the idea of a talking bathtub that took me on a strange adventure. So I did not tell her about it, and the tub and I are still friends!

The End

Here is a picture of me on my adventure with the tub.

drawn by _____

Think about a food you do not like. What if you were that food? How would you feel if no one else liked you? What could you say or do to make people like you? Write a story as if YOU were that food. When you are done, draw a picture to go with your story.

_____

_____

_____

_____

_____

_____

_____

_____

_____

_____

_____

_____

_____

_____

_____

_____

_____

_____

_____

_____

_____

_____

_____

_____

_____

_____

_____

_____

_____

_____

_____

The End

drawn by _____

What if you had one wish, but you couldn't use the wish for yourself? What if you could only wish for something for somebody else? What would you wish for? Why? Write a story about someone who has that wish. When you are done, draw a picture to go with your story.

_____

_____

_____

_____

_____

_____

_____

_____

_____

_____

_____

_____

_____

_____

_____

_____

_____

_____

_____

_____

_____

_____

_____

_____

_____

_____

_____

_____

The End

drawn by _____

What if you and your best friend switched bodies for a day? What would your day be like? What would your best friend think of his or her day? Write a story as if that really happened! When you are done, draw a picture to go with your story.

_____

_____

_____

_____

_____

_____

_____

_____

_____

_____

_____

_____

_____

_____

_____

_____

_____

_____

_____

_____

_____

_____

_____

_____

_____

_____

_____

_____

_____

_____

_____

The End

drawn by _____

What if the letter "S" disappeared? How would that change the world? How would it change your life? There would be no "shoes," for example. Everyone would walk around with "hoes" strapped to their feet! "School" would be "cool" . . . sort of. "Spain" would be nothing more than a "pain" to visit!

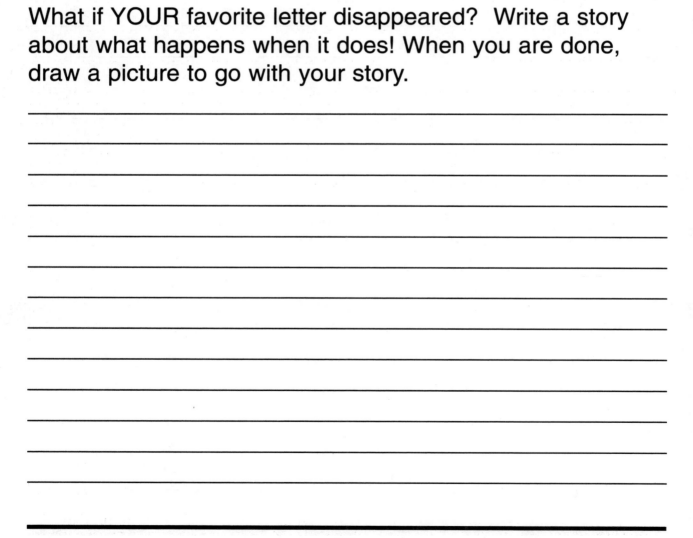

What if YOUR favorite letter disappeared? Write a story about what happens when it does! When you are done, draw a picture to go with your story.

_____

_____

_____

_____

_____

_____

_____

_____

_____

_____

_____

_____

_____

The End

drawn by

On the following pages, write your own stories. You can write about anything you choose! Don't forget to draw a picture to go with each story. You can use more paper if you need to.

_____

_____

_____

_____

_____

_____

_____

_____

_____

_____

_____

_____

_____

_____

_____

_____

_____

draun by

drawn by ✏️ _____

_____

_____

_____

_____

_____

_____

_____

_____

_____

_____

_____

_____

_____

_____

drawn by _____

On the lines below, write all about yourself. This is called an author biography, and you are the author of this book! You can include your age, what you look like, where you live, and what you like to do. In the space provided, you can paste a picture of yourself, or draw a self-portrait.

ABOUT THE AUTHOR

_____

_____

_____

_____

_____

_____

_____

_____

_____

_____